Our Emotions and Behaviour

to
P...y!

Written ... and ...ini

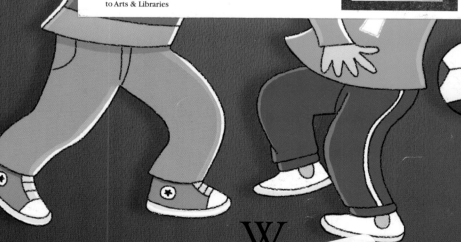

W

Finn was in Mr Hare's class.
Finn was not very kind.
He cared mostly about himself.
He didn't help Ahmed when he felt ill.

He didn't help Lily hang up her bag.

At playtime everyone played football.
But Finn **didn't play nicely**.
He knocked Freddy over.

He pushed Molly out of the way.

Molly said Finn was **unkind**.
She said he should play nicely.

But Finn didn't want to play nicely.
He said playing nicely was boring!

Everyone was **cross** with Finn.
They told Mr Hare about it.
Mr Hare had a good idea.

Mr Hare said Finn would be Jake's **buddy**. Jake was new at school.

Mr Hare said Finn should spend the day with Jake and **help him**.

12

But Finn **didn't want** to be Jake's buddy. He didn't look after him at all. He didn't help him hang up his coat.

Finn didn't show Jake round the school. Jake got lost. He was **very upset**.

Molly told Finn that Jake had a bad start to school because of him.
She said Finn was **not nice.**
Finn did **not feel** happy.

At playtime no one played with Finn.
They said he was **too unkind**.
They said he didn't play nicely.
Finn was **sad**.
Mr Hare had a talk with him.

Mr Hare said that if Finn wanted friends, he needed to **play nicely**. He said Finn should try to **make things right**.

Finn thought about it.

He said he would tell everyone he was **sorry for being unkind.**
He said he would offer to **help** Jake.
He said he would try to play nicely, too.
Mr Hare said those were all good ideas.

Finn told everyone
he was sorry.

20

He helped Jake hang up his coat.

He showed him round the school.

21

At playtime everyone played basketball. Finn was **very kind**. He gave Molly his gloves to keep her warm.

He helped Jake score a point.
He **played really nicely**, too.

Jake said Finn was the **best buddy** ever! Finn decided he liked being a buddy.

He liked playing nicely, too.

Playing nicely wasn't boring at all!

Can you tell the story of what happens when Henry and Amy decorate their pots?

How do you think Henry felt when Amy snatched the paint? How does he feel at the end?

A note about sharing this book

The *Our Emotions and Behaviour* series has been developed to provide a starting point for further discussion on children's feelings and behaviour, both in relation to themselves and to other people.

I Don't Want to Play Nicely!
This story looks at the importance of playing considerately with other children. It points out the importance of being aware of others' needs and being prepared to help rather than ignore others' difficulties.

Storyboard puzzle
The wordless storyboard on pages 26 and 27 provides an opportunity for speaking and listening. Children are encouraged to tell the story illustrated in the panels: Henry and Amy are painting their pots until Amy snatches the green paint from Henry, spilling it on the table. Henry is upset that he cannot finish his pot, and a class mate comes to his rescue, telling off Amy for snatching the paint. Amy feels bad for upsetting Henry and gets some more green paint. Finally, the three classmates finish decorating their pots together.

How to use the book
The book is designed for adults to share with either an individual child, or a group of children, and as a starting point for discussion.

The book also provides visual support and repeated words and phrases to build confidence in children who are starting to read on their own.

Before reading the story
Choose a time to read when you and the children are relaxed and have time to share the story.

Spend time looking at the illustrations and talk about what the book may be about before reading it together.

After reading, talk about the book with the children:

- What was it about? Have the children ever felt cross because someone has not played nicely and perhaps spoiled a game?

- Have they ever been mean to others? Invite them to relate their experiences. How did the other children respond to them? How did they put things right?

- Has anyone been inconsiderate or unkind to them at school or during a game? How did they feel? What did they do about it? Did someone, e.g. a teacher or an older child, help them to resolve the problem?

Ask the children to talk about the importance of playing nicely with others. How does it improve a game? Point out that not playing nicely can spoil a game for others but also for themselves too.

To Isabelle, William A, George, William G, Max, Emily,
Leo, Caspar, Felix and Phoebe –S.G.

Franklin Watts
First published in Great Britain in 2017 by The Watts Publishing Group

Text © Franklin Watts 2017
Illustrations © Emanuela Carletti and Desideria Guicciardini 2017

The rights of Emanuela Carletti and Desideria Guicciardini
to be identified as the illustrators of this Work have been asserted
in accordance with the Copyright, Designs and Patents Act, 1988.

ISBN (hardback) 978 1 4451 5200 4
ISBN (paperback) 978 1 4451 5201 1

Editor: Jackie Hamley
Designer: Peter Scoulding

Printed in China

FSC
www.fsc.org
MIX
Paper from
responsible sources
FSC® C104740

Franklin Watts
An imprint of
Hachette Children's Group
Part of The Watts Publishing Group
Carmelite House
50 Victoria Embankment
London EC4Y 0DZ

An Hachette UK Company
www.hachette.co.uk

www.franklinwatts.co.uk